# THE HALVERGATE FLEET: PAST & PRESENT

## Sheila Hutchinson

GW00758871

Front Cover Photograph.
Elsie High, nee Cannon, wife of marshman Bertie High, on the marshes near High's mill with their dogs. One of the dogs was called Bob but the other Rover was called by several names because whenever a hare was shot it would eat it. The mill was pumping, working with four cloth sails when the photograph was taken in 1944. The dyke is clearly visible on the right of the photograph and ripples caused by the pumping can be seen. Photograph kindly supplied by Mr Bertie High.

Back Cover Photograph.
Swans on the Halvergate Fleet in 1961. Photograph supplied by Mr Brian Grint.

# THE HALVERGATE FLEET : PAST & PRESENT

ISBN 0-9541683-0-5


Published
by
Sheila & Paul Hutchinson
7, Colman Avenue,
Stoke Holy Cross.
Norwich.
Norfolk
NR14 8NA
e-mail address:-
sheila@hutchson.freeserve.co.uk



Printed
By
RPD Litho Printers
Gorleston
Norfolk

# THE HALVERGATE FLEET : PAST & PRESENT

## Acknowledgements:

It has been a great pleasure to meet up with many people who have lived, worked, and played on and around the Halvergate Fleet, having been warmly welcomed into many of their homes for a good old yarn about how it once was. I wish to thank them all.
I wish to express many thanks to the following people and organizations for their help in providing valuable information and permission to reproduce photographs, information and tales for this Book:-
Mr Peter Allard. Mr Ray Brister. Mr Roy Carr. Mr Jack Carter. Mrs Janet Church (nee High). Mrs Margaret Durham (nee Webster). Mr Trevor Dyble. Mr Sid Gibbs. Mr Brian Grint. Mrs Dorothy Hanton (nee Carter). Mr Bertie High. Mr Ernest Hewitt. Mr Percy Hewitt. Ms. Amanda Jaques of The Norfolk Windmills Trust. Mr Billy Lacey. Mr & Mrs Bob & Violet Mace. Mr Ivan Mace. Mrs Phylis Neave. Mr David Pyett. Mr Richard Seago. Mr Arthur C Smith. Mrs Daphne Thorpe. Mr & Mrs Wes and Stella Tooley. Mr John Willimott. Eastern Daily Press, Eastern Evening News, Great Yarmouth Mercury, Public Record Office.

Special thanks go to Paul Hutchinson for all his encouragement, help with research, scanning of photographs, and the typing of the book for publication.

## About the Author:

I lived at the Berney Arms hamlet from 1946 to 1963 and the marsh folk on the Halvergate Fleet were our nearest neighbours and were occasionally seen on the Berney Arms station. In the year 2000 I wrote the book 'Berney Arms: Past & Present'.

## Disclaimer:

Much of the information herein is from people's memories and therefore it may contain some errors as often people's memories are less accurate than they believe, and often people contradict each other. I have tried to check the accuracy but I apologise for any errors that may be present, and I cannot accept responsibility for the consequences of any errors and omissions.

THE HALVERGATE FLEET : PAST & PRESENT

Dedicated to my first grandson, James Callum Black born 17th June 2000, and for all our children to let them know how their ancestors once lived.

# THE HALVERGATE FLEET : PAST & PRESENT

## Contents

**BIBLIOGRAPHY & REFERENCES:**
Martin George, The Land Use, Ecology and Conservation of Broadland. 1992, ISBN 185341 0470
Tom Williamson, The Norfolk Broads: A Landscape Survey. 1997.
Martin Ewans, The Battle for the Broads. 1992, ISBN 0861380924.
Brian Grint, The Halvergate Chronicles,
Sheila Hutchinson, Berney Arms: Past & Present, 2000.
A.J. Ward, The mills of the Fleet, in East Anglian Mag. 1963, p.252.
A.J. Ward, unpublished notes, held by the Norfolk Windmills Trust.
Arthur C. Smith, Drainage Windmills of the Norfolk Marshes, 1990.
Census Records 1841,1851,1861,1871,1881,1891, held at Norfolk Records Office.
Kelly's Directories, 1900, 1904, 1908, 1916, 1937
White's Directories, 1845, 1854, 1864, 1883
Harrod's Directory, 1868.

# THE HALVERGATE FLEET : PAST & PRESENT

## INTRODUCTION.

The Halvergate Fleet is a relict natural saltwater creek, running from Halvergate, and Wickhampton, through the marshes to Breydon Water. It is about 4 miles long. The source of the Fleet is not far from the Red Lion Public House on Marsh Road in Halvergate.

Land submergence and elevation thousands of years ago altered the coastline of East Anglia and the area now occupied by the marshes of the lower Bure, Yare and Waveney were once part of a shallow bay or estuary. The gradual elevation of the land combined with the formation of a sandbank at what has become Great Yarmouth and the silting up of the estuary has created the marshlands. Embankment of the rivers probably began around the twelfth century and helped in the reclamation of the marshland. In the thirteenth century the sea level was about thirteen feet lower than it is today.

As the silting of the estuary occurred natural creeks and rivulets were formed which drained away the salt waters at low tide. The Halvergate Fleet is the longest one of the many naturally formed creeks to be found across the marshlands.

When embanking the Fleet, as with the rivers and other natural creeks, the people would probably have built two banks or 'walls' along either side running the full length to Breydon Water. The inner wall was known as the summer wall and held back heavy summer rain, the second wall was about 20 yards away and was known as the winter wall. The area between the two walls, known as the Rands or the Ronds, would flood to a depth of about two feet at winter times.

As the marshland was reclaimed from the estuary it was allocated to existing parishes. The marshes bordering the Halvergate Fleet were for the most part allocated to the adjacent parishes of Halvergate and Wickhampton, but some areas were allocated to distant parishes and so we had a detached South Walsham, a detached Beighton and a detached Freethorpe all bordering the Fleet.

In the earliest days the marshes were probably used as rough grazing for local cattle but by the eighteenth century cattle droves from Scotland and Wales brought cattle by the thousands to these marshes, which were considered to provide some of the best grazing in the country. To assist in draining the marshes, other dykes and smaller drains were cut across the marshes and a number of drainage mills were built close to the Halvergate Fleet to drain water from the man-made dykes into the Fleet and then into Breydon Water. About 18 miles of main drains across the marshes drain into the Fleet. A sluice gate was also constructed at the end of the Fleet at Breydon Water to control the draining of the Fleet water into Breydon and to prevent the tidal waters entering the Fleet dyke.

The history of the earliest mills is uncertain, and although some drainage mills were probably built long before, the earliest clear documentation is Faden's Map of Norfolk published in 1797 which shows 6 drainage mills on or close to the Halvergate Fleet. In 1884 there was a total of eight drainage pumps, seven of which were windmills and one a steam pump.

Marsh-houses were also constructed close to most of the mills. The houses were occupied by the marshmen, who operated the mills, and their families. The marshmen did much more

6

# THE HALVERGATE FLEET : PAST & PRESENT

than operate the drainage mills. They were also responsible for tending the cattle, clearing the dykes and drains, repairing the fences, mowing thistles and generally looking after the marshland. A marshman's wage was often low and most of them supplemented their income by shooting wildfowl and game, of which there was once plenty on the marshes, and by keeping chickens, geese and their own cows.

The mills and marsh houses were remote from the villages and the embanked Fleet wall was probably the main track between Halvergate and Great Yarmouth for many centuries.

In 1831 the 'Turnpike Trust' opened the Yarmouth to Acle 'New Road' and 'Branch Road' joining Halvergate to the New Road was also opened. A brick tollhouse and tollgate was erected across Marsh Road near Wooden Hut Corner in Halvergate. The Toll collector in 1841 was listed as Robert Brooks, aged 55.

Prior to this time the people of Halvergate wishing to get to Great Yarmouth would have used the track across the marshes now known as the Weavers Way to Berney Arms and then along the river wall, or alternatively go along the Fleet Bank to Breydon Water and then along the Breydon wall. The new roadways probably made little difference at that time to lives of the people who lived in the marsh houses on the Fleet.

The children of the marshmen, having been born and brought up on the marshes, would help out and soon themselves were capable of doing a marshman's job. So the job as a marshman was often handed down through the family and the same family was often found at the same marsh house for several generations. The marshmen's daughters often married the sons of other nearby marshmen and so we find that many of the marshfolk were related.

The area originally drained by one pump was referred to as a level and the responsibility for draining the level originally fell on the landowner or landowners. Various landowners often made agreements to share the costs of the drainage and eventually Drainage Boards were formed by order of the Ministry of Agriculture and Fisheries. The Land Drainage Act of 1930 provided for the establishment of Catchment Boards, and the East Suffolk & Norfolk Catchment Board was formed in 1931. The Halvergate Fleet Internal Drainage Board was formed in 1934. The Lower Bure, Halvergate Fleet and Acle Marshes Internal Drainage Board was formed from three separate drainage boards in 1945.

After the Electric pump was built at Breydon the drainage windmills on the Fleet became redundant and life began to change for the marshmen. The Fleet was becoming a low level drain and the surrounding marshes became drier. Many of the wading birds and wildfowl disappeared from the marshes. Many landowners in the 1960's and 70's began converting their marshes to arable farming which was more profitable than grazing cattle, and several marshes around the Acle New Road to the north of the Fleet were converted. Most of the marshmen left the marshes and the houses on the Fleet became empty and were sold off as private dwellings and holiday homes.

The Broads Authority was established in 1979 and in later years was able to help prevent the arable conversion of many of the grazing marshes by the Fleet.

The RSPB acquired some marshes at Berney Arms to the south of the Fleet in 1986 and restored them to shallow flooded conditions to attract the wildfowl and wading birds back to the marshes.

## 1. STEAM MILL
Marsh Road Halvergate TG462069
This was marked on the 1883 OS map as 'Corn Mill and Draining Pump'.
It is believed to have been a steam mill driving a paddle wheel, and built for Squire Gilbert in the 1860's and was for draining the Hall level into the Fleet. It was also used for milling cake. It was a red brick building with a slate roof.
Mr Thomas Kidner Esq. was a major landowner in Halvergate and was listed in the 1904 and 1908 Kelly's Directories as owner of Halvergate Hall. In the 1916 directory his widow was living at the Hall. The Kidner family owned the steam mill, and Myrus Sutton bought it from them when he took over Halvergate Hall.
There was a wooden house near to the steam mill, where Marsh Road, Branch Road and Stone Road meet and this was referred to as Wooden Hut Corner. This wooden house was occupied for some time by the Mallet family.
After a wide dyke was made from the Engine Carr to Stones Mill the Steam mill was no longer required, and the steam mill stopped working in the 1920's.
The last known operator was 'Chummy' Mallett who lived in the The City, Halvergate.
The boiler was removed in the early 1930's according to Peter Allard's research, and the building was demolished in the early 1950's, according to Ray Brister who recalls playing in the old buildings as a child. Other reports, however, suggest it was demolished during the war years.
No photographs of the steam mill have been found.
In the Halvergate censuses we find the following entries:
*Note my additional comments, and information which was **not** in the censuses, are shown in ( ) brackets throughout.*
There was no Engine driver listed in 1861, confirming the mill was built after 1861.
1871 Entry No 103

| | | |
|---|---|---|
| Alfred Mallet | 44 | Engine driver |
| Hannah Mallet | 43 | wife |
| Maria Mallet | 18 | |
| Alfred Mallet | 15 | |

1881 Entry No 45. Marsh Road.

| | | |
|---|---|---|
| Alfred Mallet | 54 | Engine driver |
| Hannah Mallet | 53 | wife |
| Fred Lovell | 7 | grandson |
| Name not clear! | 3 | granddaughter |

1891 Entry No 54. The City.

| | | |
|---|---|---|
| Alfred Mallet | 34 | Steam Engine Driver (son of above Alfred) |
| Anna Mallet | 30 | wife |
| Alfred Mallet | 9 | |
| Maria Mallet | 8 | |
| Frances Mallet | 4 | |

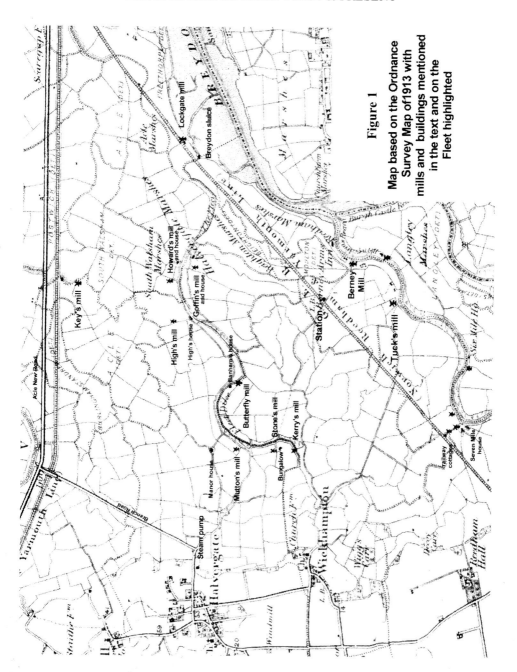

Figure 1

Map based on the Ordnance
Survey Map of 1913 with
mills and buildings mentioned
in the text and on the
Fleet highlighted

**Figure 2 Kerry's Mill in full working order in March 1944.**
**Photo supplied by Peter Allard.**

**Figure 3 Kerry's mill in June 1974. Courtesy of Arthur C Smith.**

**Figure 4 Shooting Party with Joe Kerry second from the right.
Photo supplied by Margaret Durham.**

## 2. KERRY'S MILL Wickhampton Marshes. TG441056

This Mill was owned by the Kerry family, who lived at Church Farm in Wickhampton, hence the name, however, it is often called **Stone's mill** and is marked on 1996 OS map as Stone's Mill. The marshman Wes Stone was responsible for both Carter's (also called Stone's) mill and Kerry's mill in the 1920's and through to the early 1940's, hence the confusion with names.

According to my grandfather, Henry Hewitt, nicknamed 'Yoiton', Joe Kerry owned and worked the mill. Joe Kerry lived at Church Farm Wickhampton , and was a member of the Drainage Board for many years.

The mill at this location was first marked on the 1884 O.S. map, but an earlier mill had stood some distance away at approximately TG433054 and was shown on both the 1797 Faden's map and the 1826 Bryant's map. It is probable that the former mill, or mills, were cloth-sail mills.

There is no indication on the 1843 Tithe Map for Wickhampton of any mills at either of these locations, so Kerry's mill must have been built sometime between 1843 and 1883. The land where Kerry's mill was to later appear was, in 1843, owned by Rev John Emmit Willshire and was worked by a Mr John Hewitt.

**Figure 5 Church Farm Wickhampton. Photo supplied by Margaret Durham.**

The 'English bond' brick Tower of Kerry's mill is still standing, now totally derelict with no sails and no cap and is tilted to the north. It was a 4 storey high, tarred red brick tower with a Norfolk boat-shaped cap and a 6-vane fantail. It had patent sails and an external double scoopwheel and drained about 200 acres. We cannot be sure who built it but some sources suggest Barnes, and others say it was built by William Hewitt, with the brickwork by Mutton of Halvergate and castings by Hindle of Reedham.

The mill was last operated in about 1947/8 by Fred 'Orkshire' Carter.

During WW II in 1943 an aeroplane (Lancaster) crash-landed on the marsh next to Kerry's mill.

No **marsh-house** is shown alongside this mill on the old maps (although a building was marked at TG442053 on the 1883 OS map and on the 1843 Tithe Map of Wickhampton, and this may have been a marsh-house at one time.) However, we have found no evidence in the Wickhampton censuses of a marshman who could have lived nearby this mill, and it is quite possible that the marshman living next to Carter's mill looked after both mills, as Wes Stone did between the two World Wars.

We find the following information about **Church Farm** and the **Kerry family**.

Mr R. Dunthorne bought Church Farm in the early 1980's.

Mr Joe Kerry had Church Farm in the 1940's and 50's.

Kelly's 1937 Directory lists for Wickhampton Fred William Kerry, farmer at Church Farm.

Kelly's 1916 Directory lists for Wickhampton Frank Kerry, farmer.

Kelly's 1908 Directory lists for WickHampton Frank Kerry, Farmer at Church Farm.

Kelly's 1904 Directory lists for Wickhampton Joseph Houchen Kerry, Farmer at Church Farm.

1891 Wickhampton Census

| | | |
|---|---|---|
| Joseph Kerry | 55(?) | Farmer |
| Jane Kerry | 47 | wife |
| Edward Kerry | 21 | |
| Henrietta Kerry | 19 | |
| Etc. | | |

1883 Kelly's Directory for Wickhampton lists Joseph Kerry, Farmer at Church Farm

1881 Wickhampton Census

Entry No. 196

| | | |
|---|---|---|
| Joseph Kerry | 49 | Farmer 244 acres |
| Jane Kerry | 37 | wife |
| George Kerry | 14 | |
| Edward Kerry | 11 | |
| Sarah Jane Kerry | 10 | |
| Henrietta Kerry | 9 | |
| Walter Kerry | 8 | |
| Fred Kerry | 7 | |

| Frank Kerry | 5 | |
| Lucy Kerry | 7 | |
| Isabella Heoward | (?) | Governess |
| Sarah Ann Stamp | (?) | Dom Servant |

1871 Wickhampton Census
Entry No. 5 Church Farm

| Joseph Kerry | 32 | Farmer 188 acres |
| Jane Kerry | 27 | wife |
| George Kerry | 5 | |
| Cubitt Kerry | 4 | |
| Alice Kerry | 2 | |
| Edward Kerry | 1 | |
| Sarah J Bessy Kerry | 4mths | |
| Susan ?? | 21 | dairymaid |
| Mary Turner | 15 | nursemaid |

1868 Harrod's Directory lists for Wickhampton Joseph Kerry, Farmer

1861 Wickhampton Census
Entry No 5 Church Farm

| Josiah Wiffen | 52 | Farmer 300 acres (buried at Wickhampton) |
| Ann Wiffen | 53 | wife |
| Annie Wiffen | 21 | |
| Harriet Cockeral | 54 | servant |
| Elizabeth Clark | 21 | |

**Figure 6 Joe Kerry.**
**Photo supplied by Margaret Durham.**

Figure 7 Carter's (Stone's) Mill in full working order with the bungalow to the left and Kerry's mill in the distance to the right. Photo supplied by Billy Lacey.

## 3. CARTER'S MILL. TG441058 Halvergate Parish.

This was also known as **STONE'S MILL**.
It stands on Baker's level, and was first shown on Faden's map of 1797. It was also shown on Bryant's map as the 'Halvergate Mill', and was also shown on the 1839 Halvergate Tithe Award map. In 1842 the land where this mill stood belonged to a Maria Nesbitt and was occupied, or worked, by Ben Howard according to the Tithe Apportionment of that date. Ben Howard was living at the Manor House, according to the 1841 census.

The mill was later owned by Myrus Sutton for many years, and was operated by Leonard Carter until he died in 1918, then by Wes Stone, and later by Fred Carter, nicknamed 'Orkshire'. Fred was one of Leonard Carter's sons.

The mill was 3 storeys high and may have been built, or rebuilt, by Barnes of Yarmouth but had machinery from an earlier mill. It drove an external scoopwheel.
It was a Brick tower with patent sails but may have previously been cloth-sailed. The sails turned anti-clockwise with 48 shutters per sail. It had an 8 bladed fantail and a boat-shaped cap with no gallery. The cogs were made with apple-wood and needed regular replacement, and the other internal wooden parts were made from ash and pine. The brass ends required frequent greasing as it got very hot.
The mill was last operated in 1948 by Fred Carter, and the mill was demolished in the early 1950's. The exact site is difficult to locate with few remains but it was very close to the bungalow.

### Marsh Bungalow at TG441058.
This is a bungalow, which is unusual for a marsh cottage.
No dwelling was shown on the Halvergate map of 1839, but a building is shown on the 1883 and the 1907 O.S maps. The bungalow is built in brick with a tile roof. It was tarred black, like the mill, until it was sold as a private holiday home.

### Some Occupants:
Leonard Carter was marshman in the early 1900's until he died during the flue epidemic in 1918. His wife was Henrietta, nee Hewitt, known as Hettie, and they had 8 children, one of them George drowned in a dyke. Two of the children, Walter and Fred, tried to make a wooden plane and tried to fly it off the top of Carter's mill. It just crashed into the ground and both of them were lucky to survive.
Wes Stone then moved in here in 1918, after he returned from sea. Wes had a son, Wes Stone junior, who also lived and worked here on the marshes. Wes Tooley, a grandson to Wes Stone, also lived here with his grandfather until 1940 when he enlisted. Tom 'Teaser' Carter took Wes Tooley's place for a brief period until he too went into the forces.

Figure 8 Carter's Mill in full working order. Photo supplied by Peter Allard.

Figure 9 Bungalow near Carter's Mill standing empty 31st May 1969.
Photo supplied by Peter Allard

**Figure 10 Fred Carter on the marsh track near the bungalow in1951.
Photo supplied by Daphne Thorpe.**

**Figure 11 Fred and Alice Carter 1973 celebrating a wedding anniversary after they
had moved from the marshes. Photo from Daphne Thorpe.**

THE HALVERGATE FLEET : PAST & PRESENT

Fred Carter, a son of Leonard, had worked for both Myrus and Ben Sutton as a pigman and a drover. He was nicknamed 'Orkshire' and he moved into the bungalow as the marshman in late 1940's, and stayed till the early 1960's, when he left and moved to Blofield Heath. 'Orkshire' got his nickname because whenever he was asked what he wanted to eat he always replied 'Orkshire' pudding whether it was morning, noon or night.

His wife was Alice, nee Hewitt, a great granddaughter to Edward and Esther Hewitt who were once at Howard's mill marsh house.

Billy Lacey moved here after Fred Carter left, in about 1963-4, and was here till 1968.

The bungalow was empty for a short time, and was later sold to a Mr David Talkes and used as a holiday home.

The following information has been found in the Halvergate censuses and directories.

1937 Kelly's Directory Wesley Stone cowkeeper.

1916, 1908, and 1904 Kelly's directories list a Mr Fred Carter as cowkeeper.

The following may relate to the marsh bungalow, but we cannot be certain since the date of the bungalow is uncertain.

1891 Halvergate Census
Entry76. The Marsh House.

| John Carter | 70 | Marshman |
| Sarah Carter | 66 | wife |
| Edith Carter | 15 | visitor |
| Ann Hunt | 15 | visitor |

1881 Halvergate Census
Entry No. 50 Marsh Road Marsh house

| John Carter | 62 | Marshman |
| Ann Carter | 57 | wife |

1871 Halvergate Census
Entry No. 97

| John Carter | 52 | marshman |
| Sarah Carter | 47 | wife |
| Fred Carter | 23 | Ag Lab |
| Maria Carter | 19 | |

1861 Halvergate Census
Entry No 113

| John Carter | 42 | marshman |
| Sarah Carter | 38 | wife |
| Fred Carter | 13 | |
| Maria Carter | 9 | |

1854 White's Directory lists a John Carter as Farmer.

**Figure 13 Stella Tooley, nee Wills
in the 1930's before she married
Wes Tooley.
Photo from Stella Tooley.**

**Figure 12 Wes Stone.
Photo supplied by Ray Brister.**

## WES TOOLEY

Wes Stone moved to the marsh bungalow after returning from sea, where he had been a fisherman, in 1918. His wife was called Tabitha and after she died her niece, Millie Read from Tunstall moved in and became Wes Stone's housekeeper.

Wes Tooley, who is now 88 years old, left school in 1927, aged 14, and went to live with his grandfather, Wes Stone, at the marsh bungalow and worked for him looking after cows, calves and chickens. He worked alongside his uncle, Wes Stone junior.

They had their own cows. The cream was separated from the milk and made into butter and the milk was used for rearing the calves. The butter was taken in a hamper across the marshes and then by train from Berney Arms station to the co-op in Great Yarmouth. The return rail fare from Berney to Yarmouth Vauxhall was five old pence in those days.

There was about 1,000 acres on different levels to look after. The majority of these levels were owned by Ben Sutton, who lived at the Manor House Freethorpe, Ben's son Myrus, who lived at Halvergate Hall, and Jack Key who farmed from Tunstall. Ben and Myrus had Irish stores delivered to Reedham station by train from Liverpool and the cattle drovers Jack Edwards and Enoch Bracey took the cattle through the roads to Wickhampton then onto the marshes where they were tended by the marshmen and stayed until the drovers took them to Norwich Market to be sold. Myrus Sutton had some marshes by the Breydon sluice. He kept colts there. They referred to them as 'water-bellies' because when they walked you could hear their stomachs slushing. Thistle mowing was piecework paid at one shilling an acre. During the 1920's and 1930's, when unemployment was very high, many people came out to work on the marshes, slubbing out the dykes and thistle topping. These unemployed people were paid only six old pence an acre and were happy with that as there was no other employment.

Wes Tooley on some Saturdays would look after Mutton's mill when Fred Mutton went to the market.

When Kerry's, Carter's and Mutton's mills were all working together they would cause the marshes by High's mill to flood and James Thomas High would set his sails to signal them to stop pumping.

In 1938 the Fleet Dyke was slubbed out from end to end.

For Dyke drawing they were paid by the rod; three shillings a rod before WWII, but after the war they were paid by the chain.

To shorten a journey across the marshes Wes Tooley was taught to pole vault across the wide dykes.

Shooting parties often came down to the marshes: the Gurneys, the Barcleys and Captain Fielding of the Queen's Flight were a few notables who went there. At that time there was thousands of geese and ducks, the flight path for the geese was from Scroby and they flew in a V-formation.

Coal was delivered in bags to Wooden Hut Corner, on Stone Road, Halvergate and Wes would go to collect it with the horse and cart.

They used water from the roof and also got churns of water from the Red Lion Public house in Halvergate, using the horse and cart to collect them.

Hurricane lamps were used for lights outside and in the cattle sheds at night, and candles and mantle lamps were used indoors.

Washing was done in a copper with a fire underneath, and cooking was done on a coalfire cooking range. They also had an open coalfire.

Wes Tooley remembers when the Fleet Dyke froze up. He skated all the way to the Breydon sluice and back along the frozen dyke. He had a pair of skates that screwed into the heels and soles of his boots, and he still has them to this day.

Wes Tooley went into the forces in 1940, and Tom 'Teaser' Carter moved into the bungalow replacing Wes Tooley, until Tom also went into the armed forces.

Figure 14 Tom (Teaser) Carter & Arthur Tooley near Carter's mill in the mid 1930's. Tom worked for Wes Stone for a time and Arthur worked for East Anglian Real Property Co Ltd who owned some of the marshes between Wickhampton and Reedham. Supplied by Wes Tooley.

Figure 15 Studio portrait of Wes Tooley in July 1936. Photo supplied by Wes and Stella Tooley.

## BILLY LACEY

Billy Lacey lived in the bungalow in the 1960's .The bungalow had four rooms. Leading off from the sitting room there was a conservatory and an alley way to the dairy.

There was no mains electricity but they had an electric generator, which was used for the lights and the television.

There was no mains water and rainwater was collected off the roof into a tank and they also fetched churns of water from Halvergate using their Landrover.

The toilet was outside. There was no refuse collection and all rubbish was buried.
Billy was a marshman and had his own cows, which he used for rearing calves. He also had some sheep. Billy had a dog named 'Fly' which helped him to round up the cattle and sheep on the marshes.
Billy moved out off the bungalow in 1968 and moved to Marsh Road Halvergate but continued as a marshman.
The bungalow was sold to Mr David Talkes and is used as a holiday home.

When 'Orkshire' Carter lived at the bungalow in the 1950's, 'Orkshire', like Henry Everson at the other end of the Fleet, had an electric generator which would boil a kettle, work a television and a light. Once switched on from indoors it would run continually until the light was turned off.

**Figure 16 Billy Lacey's dog 'Fly' helped to round up cattle and sheep.**
**Photo supplied by Billy Lacey.**

**Figure 17 Billy Lacey by the Fleet in 1991. Courtesy of EDP.**

**Figure 18 Mutton's Mill in full working order. Photo supplied by Peter Allard.**

**4. MUTTON'S MILL**    TG442064 Halvergate Parish.
This was also known as **MANOR HOUSE MILL.**

**Figure 19 Mutton's mill in September 1973. Courtesy of Arthur C Smith**

Bryant's Map of 1826 shows **'Fellows Farm & Mill'** at this approximate location, but another mill had existed nearby in 1769, and was also shown on a map of 1803.
This earlier mill was probably demolished sometime in the 1820's or 1830's when it was replaced by a mill some 200m to the SW.
Note the name 'Fellows' above must refer to the family of Robert Fellowes Esq. of Shotesham Park who was listed in White's directory of 1845 and in Kelly's directory of 1908 as Lord of the Manor and was a major landowner in Halvergate. He owned the land and mill in 1842 at the time of the Tithe Apportionment.
The mill stands on what was once called the Frothelmes Level and was a tarred red brick tower with 4 patent sails, which turned anti-clockwise. The sails were double shuttered with 8 bays, with 3 shutters each, giving 48 per sail. It had a 6 bladed fantail and a boat-shaped cap.
It is 4 storeys high, with a height of about 40 ft to the curb. The base diameter is 24 ft, and the curb diameter 14 ft. It had an internal scoop wheel, 15.5 feet in diameter, with 18 inch wide paddles.
It is possible that it was built or rebuilt built by Stolworthy of Yarmouth.
It was last worked in about 1947 by Fred Mutton and was derelict for several years with 4 sails.

The mill was owned by Lady Stracey until it was sold off.
Paul Reynolds and David High took the mill over in 1974. Some repairs were done in 1976, and a new cap and fantail was fitted in 1984, and one set of sails was fitted in 1998.


## MANOR HOUSE          TG441067

Bryant's Map of 1826 shows buildings marked as 'Fellows Farm ' at this approximate location, and a house and other outbuildings is marked on the 1839 Halvergate Tithe map. The house is built of brick with 18 inch wide walls, and had downstairs two large front rooms, kitchen, pantry and a dairy, and upstairs five bedrooms. The house was said to be a 'double dweller' at the front and a 'single dweller' at the back, according to the unpublished notes of AJ Ward who had spoken to Fred Mutton junior in 1962. This arrangement meant that two rooms could be let and the occupants had their own entrance doors. This may be consistent with 1881 census where there are two separate entries for the related Howard and Mutton families. Fred Mutton kept a few cows of his own and they fetched their water in churns from Halvergate, had no electricity and used candles and Tilly lamps for lighting. The house is still standing today and now has it's own electricity generator.

Occupants:
After the Mutton family left the marshes the house has been occupied by several people including a Mr David Hart, a Mr Colin Moseley, and lastly a Dr King, who still lives there.

The following information has been found documented.

| | | |
|---|---|---|
| 1937 Kelly's Directory | Fred Howard Mutton, marshman & cow-keeper | |
| 1916 Kelly's Directory | Fred H. Mutton, marshman & cowkeeper, The Marsh Farm | |
| 1908 Kelly's Directory | Fred Mutton, cowkeeper | |
| 1904 Kelly's Directory | Fred Mutton, cow-keeper | |
| 1900 Kelly's Directory | Fred Mutton, cow-keeper | |

1891 Halvergate census
Entry No 115 ' On the marshes'

| | | |
|---|---|---|
| James Mutton | 50 | Marshman (he was a Bricklayer in 1881) |
| Phoebe Mutton | 50 | wife |
| Fred Mutton | 21 | marshman / son   (had a middle name Howard) |
| Phoebe Mutton | 19 | (full name Phoebe Kerrison Howard Mutton later marries George Brister) |
| Nellie Mutton | 17 | (Nellie Howard Mutton later she marries James Thomas High. She dies 2 Jan 1951) |
| Roger Mutton | 15 | marshman |

1881 Halvergate Census

| | | |
|---|---|---|
| Entry No. 46 | | Marshhouse |
| Ben Howard | 79 | marsh farmer |
| Rose Waters | 16 | Domestic |

**Figure 20 Manor House standing empty in August 1970. Peter Allard Collection.**

Also
Entry No. 47

| | | |
|---|---|---|
| James Mutton | 40 | Bricklayer |
| Phoebe Mutton | 40 | wife (nee Howard) |
| Ben Mutton | 14 | scholar |
| Fred Mutton | 11 | |
| Phoebe Mutton | 9 | |
| Nellie Mutton | 7 | |
| Roger Mutton | 5 | |

1871 Halvergate Census
Entry No. 96

| | | |
|---|---|---|
| Benjamin Howard | 68 | Marsh farmer |
| Phoebe Mutton | 30 | daughter (nee Howard) |
| James Mutton | 30 | stepson bricklayer (probably should be 'Son-in-law') |
| Henry Howard Mutton | 3 | grandson |
| Fred H. Mutton | 1 | grandson |
| Louise Nichols | 17 | domestic |

1861 Halvergate census
Entry No 110

| | | |
|---|---|---|
| Ben Howard | 58 | widowed farmer |
| Sarah Callow | 68 | sister housekeeper |
| John Howard | 18 | (later at South Walsham Mill in 1871/81) |
| Sarah Callow | 29 | niece / dairymaid |
| Maria Warner? | 19 | housemaid |
| Phoebe Howard | 20 | |

1851 Halvergate Census
Entry No. 109

| | | |
|---|---|---|
| Ben Howard | 48 | widower/farmer 50acres |
| Sarah Callow | 57 | widow/housekeeper (sister) |
| Sarah Callow | 19 | niece |
| Charlotte Kirk | 18 | general sev |
| William Newson | 16 | ag lab |

1845 White's Directory for Halvergate lists Ben Howard as a farmer.
1842 Tithe Apportionment for Halvergate lists John Howard as occupant, while Ben Howard was listed as occupant for nearby Carter's (Stone's) mill.
1841 Halvergate Census

| | | |
|---|---|---|
| John Howard | 70 | marshman |
| Sarah Callow | 45 | Ind |
| Sarah Callow | 9 | |
| Benjamin Howard | 35 | Marsh farmer (was working Carter's mill at this time) |
| Phoebe Howard | 23 | |
| Phoebe Howard | 4mths | |

| Mary Eastaugh | 15 | ind |
| John Carter | 20 | |
| Sarah Mallett | 15 | |

**Figure 21 Sydney George Brister and wife Phoebe Howard Mutton at Marsh Road Halvergate. Phoebe was born and lived at Manor House. He was a wheelwright and carpenter in Halvergate. His workshop was close to the Red Lion pub. Photo supplied by Brian Grint.**

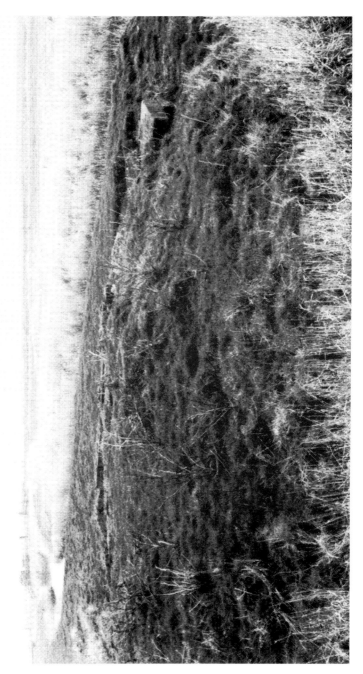

Figure 22 Site of Banham's Butterfly Mill.
Photo taken 11th March 1980 by Peter Allard.

**5. BUTTERFLY MILL** TG450063 Wickhampton Parish, Wickhampton Marshes on the southern side of the Halvergate Fleet Dyke.

The marsh and rond were once known as Gallants Marsh and Gallants Rond, and in 1843 they were owned by Sir Thomas Bowyer Smith and occupied, or used, by a Thomas Hewitt according to the Tithe Apportionment of that year. No mill or house was marked on the 1839 Tithe map. The rond was also later known as Nockler's rond.

A mill was marked on the 1884 and 1904 O.S. maps but not on the 1926 map.

It was an all white wooden Smock mill, possibly similar in appearance to the Horning smock mill.

According to grandfather, 'Yoiton', it was owned by Myrus Sutton, and was run by Bob Banham, nicknamed 'Trimmer'. 'Yoiton' also said the mill was burnt down.

Peter Allard's research indicates that the Mill was built probably about 1870, and possibly by William Hewitt, and assisted Goffin's mill drain Gilberts level. It probably had patent sails. A piece of sail found close by in January 1980 seems to confirm that it had patent sails The site of the mill and brick sluice remained till the 1980's but by 1995 it was filled in and no signs are now left.

**Figure 23 Ted Banham in 1919. He was a son of Bob 'Trimmer' Banham who lived in the house by the Butterfly mill. Photo from Ray Brister.**

**Marsh House:**

A marsh house once stood nearby, next to Hardiman's bridge. TG449065.

A building is marked at this approximate location on the 1839 Halvergate Tithe Map, even though it is just outside of the Halvergate parish boundary, but confusingly no building, is shown on the 1843 Wickhampton Tithe map!

The house does appear on the 1905 map but not on any of the later maps.

The house was wooden and no photographs or details are available. No signs of the house were present in 1970.

The house must have been demolished about the same time as the mill, probably in the early 1920's

Wes Tooley recalls that the footings of the old house were dug up and the rubble used to fill in ruts on the marsh tracks, probably in the 1930's. Wes recalls that they used to build their haystack on this site.

The bridge over the Fleet was re-made using railway sleepers when Wes Stone lived at the bungalow by Stone's mill.

## Occupants:

In light of the uncertainty about the date of the marsh house some of the earlier dated censuses listed here may refer to another building elsewhere in Wickhampton.

1891 Wickhampton Census
Entry No 161 'The Marshes'

| Robert Banham | 40 | Marshman (Robert Last Banham, a son of Last Banham) |
| Harriet Banham | 40 | wife (nee Brown) |
| Lucy Banham | 8 | |
| Harriet Banham | 4 | |

1881 Wickhampton Census
Entry No. 195

| Robert L. Banham | 31 | Marshman (Robert Last Banham, a son of Last Banham) |
| Harriet Banham | 31 | wife (nee Brown) |
| Robert L. Banham | 7 | |
| Edward Banham | 4 | |
| Harriet Banham | 10mths | |

1871 Wickhampton Census
Entry No. 4 Marsh cottage

| Robert L. Banham | 21 | Marsh Lab (Robert Last Banham, a son of Last Banham) |
| Harriet Banham | 21 | (nee Brown) |

1861 Wickhampton Census
Entry No. 4 marsh house

| Last Banham | 44 | Marshman |
| Sarah Banham | 42 | wife (nee Sarah Ann Key) |
| Robert Banham | 10 | (Robert Last Banham) |
| Daniel Banham | 8 | (Daniel Key Banham, later Lockgate marshman) |
| Benjamin Banham | 4 | (Benjamin Last Banham) |

1851 Wickhampton Census
Entry No.13

| | | |
|---|---|---|
| Last Banham | 36 | Marsh Lab. |
| Sarah Banham | 32 | wife (nee Sarah Ann Key) |
| Susan Banham | 11 | |
| Elizabeth Banham | 9 | |
| Edward Banham | 6 | |
| William Banham | 4 | |
| Robert Banham | 9mths | |

1841 Wickhampton Census

| | | |
|---|---|---|
| William Key | 63 | Ag Lab. |
| Susanna Key | 60 | wife |
| Edward Key | 17 | Ag. Lab. |
| John Briggs | 86 | Ag.lab. |
| Last Banham | 24 | |
| Sarah Banham | 22 | (nee Key) |
| Marianne Banham | 5 | |
| Susanna Banham | 2 | |

**Figure 24 High's Mill in full working order in March 1944.
Photo supplied by Peter Allard.**

**6. HIGH'S MILL** TG457072 Halvergate Parish ; Halvergate Marshes ; on the Fleet Dyke. This has been known by many names: **COTMAN'S MILL, LUBBOCK'S MILL, GILBERT'S MILL, HARDEN'S MILL** and even as Carter's Mill.

**Figure 25 High's mill 1974. Courtesy of Arthur C Smith.**

Bryant's 1826 map of Norfolk shows at this approximate location a mill, named as 'Halvergate Mill', and a nearby building, probably the marsh farmhouse, labelled as 'Hewetts'.

A mill and marsh house were also shown hereabouts on the earlier 1797 Faden's map.

This mill and the house were on Cotman's level. Cotman's level included many marshes stretching to the north and northwest, hence the name Cotman's mill. In 1842 the mill and the marshes were owned by the Shuckford's Executors.

Around 1900 a Mrs Gilbert owned the marshes, according to information from James Thomas High's record, and according to my grandfather, 'Yoiton', the mill was also owned by a Mr Harden at one time.

The mill was originally built in the 18th century according to Tom Williamson, and contains rare eighteenth century machinery, including a trundle wheel.

It was a small tarred red brick 2 storey tower mill with a boat-shaped cap and common sails which turned clockwise into the wind. It had an internal fireplace and only one window.

It had no fantail but instead a tail-pole, winch and chains for turning the sails into the wind.

It drained about 200 acres and had a 12 ft diameter external scoop wheel.

In 1922 when a new sail was required the wood was floated up the Fleet from Breydon.

It had canvas cloth sails and Bertie High said only 2 sails were issued when he was there, but he made 2 more from sacking. The sail cloths had rings attached which would slide on rods and the cloth could be pulled out over the sails with cords which were then made fast onto cleats. To furl, the cords would be let go and the cloth rolled up and hooked onto pegs at the back of the frame. Each of the four sails had to be done the same one after the other. When the strength of the wind changed the sail cloths would have to be adjusted and if the wind direction changed the cap had to be winched into the wind.

The mill was last worked by Len Carter in 1948. He dismantled the sails and tail-pole and used them for gateposts and liggers. Len Carter had previously worked the mill at Lockgate. In 1980 the mill was re-tarred and it now has a temporary aluminium cap.
The mill is now looked after by the Norfolk Windmills Trust

**Figure 26 High's Mill 1988. Courtesy Arthur C Smith.**

High's **Marsh house** TG457070 was probably built in the early 1700's, and was of brick and tiles.
Dorothy Hanton, daughter of Len Carter, recalls that when they lived there in the 1950's there were two rooms downstairs, a washhouse, and a big dairy. Upstairs there were three bedrooms, and in one of them there was a trapdoor leading to another room in the roof-space. They had no running water and used the rainwater from the roof. There was no electricity and they used Tilley lamps and primus stoves. One room had a coal-fire cooking range. Her father kept some cows to help supplement his income, something he was not able to do when he was at Lockgate mill.

Dorothy recalls a spooky incident. Her father Len was in bed and she was sat downstairs with her mother. It was after 11 o'clock at night when they heard a knock on the door. This was very unusual out there on the marshes as it was a remote place and the marshes were soaking wet by the house. Their dog took no notice as if it had heard nothing and did not stir. Dorothy went to the door but could see nothing. There was no wind to cause the noise so they sent the dog out to investigate. When the dog came back a few moments later they went outside the door to look for themselves but there was no sign of anyone or anything. The marsh was extremely wet and anyone approaching their house would have needed rubber boots and could not have disappeared very quickly. Shortly afterwards they went to bed. The next morning there was a knock on the door. The person at the door told them that Mrs High had died the night previous.

**Occupants:**
The last occupant at the marsh house was Len Carter.
Len Carter moved in to the marsh house in 1945 and he worked the mill for a couple of years. Len lived in the marsh house with his wife and daughter from about 1945 till about 1960. Len had a bike and cycled along the wall to get to Yarmouth, he also had a boat with a rope attached and if the weather was bad he would put his bike into the boat and walk along the Fleet wall pulling the boat until he got to Breydon pump, where he would tie the boat and finish his journey biking along the Breydon wall.
The house was falling down when Len Carter left, according to his daughter Dorothy Hanton. Cattle roamed about inside the derelict house, after they left, and the house was eventually demolished by Mr Lanham in about 1965 or 1966.
Bertie High and his family occupied the house from 1943 to 1945 and Bertie was the marshman who operated the mill at that time.
Bertie's father James Thomas High was the official marshman who lived here from 1900 to 1943. He and his sons operated the mill.

The following information is to be found in the censuses and directories.
1937 Kelly's Directory for Halvergate lists James Thomas High as cowkeeper / marshman.
1916 Kelly's Directory for Halvergate gives James Thomas High as cowkeeper.
Note In the 1891 census James Thomas High was living at the marsh house next to Goffin's mill (also known as Minister's) with his grandfather James Minister, and they were both listed as marshmen.

The following census information is believed to be appropriate to the marsh house by High's mill but cannot be guaranteed.

**Figure 27 High's marsh house. Top photo taken in 1930's, photo from Bertie High. Bottom when empty in 1964 from Peter Allard.**

**Figure 28 James Thomas High and wife Nellie Howard Mutton.
Photo supplied by Bertie High.**

**Figure 29 James Thomas High with daughter Margery and wife Nellie in the 1930's. The horse was called Joe. Supplied by Bertie High**

**Figure 30 Fred High on the Fleet in the 1930's. Photo from Janet Church, nee High.**

**Figure 31 Bertie High with haycart in 1930's.
Photo supplied by Bertie High.**

**Figure 32 Bertie High on the grasscutter in 1937. Courtesy of Bertie High.**

1891 Halvergate Census:
Entry 116

| | | |
|---|---|---|
| Ben Banham | 35 | marshman (son of Last Banham, & brother to Bob at the Butterfly mill, he dies in Oct 1934) |
| Francis Banham | 33 | wife (she later dies 1926) |
| Rose (unclear) | 17 | servant |

1881 Halvergate Census:
Entry No. 49 Marsh house

| | | |
|---|---|---|
| Last Banham | 64 | Marshman (dies in Jan 1889) |
| Sarah Ann Banham | 64 | wife (dies in 1893) |
| Sarah Ann Banham | 18 | |

1871 Halvergate Census:
Entry No. 98

| | | |
|---|---|---|
| Last Banham | 55 | Marsh farmer |
| Sarah Banham | 55 | (nee Sarah Ann Key) |
| Daniel Banham | 17 | Marsh man (later at Freethorpe ie. Lockgate Mill) |
| Ben Banham | 14 | |
| Sarah Banham | 8 | |

1861 Halvergate Census:
*Two possible entries for this marsh house are either* Entry No 111

| | | |
|---|---|---|
| George Thaxter | 33 | farmer |
| Ann M. Thaxter | 30 | |
| George Thaxter | 1 | |
| WilliamThaxter | 15 | nephew / marshman |

*Or* Entry No 112

| | | |
|---|---|---|
| Robert Turner | 55 | marshman (later marshman at Tunstall) |
| Prisilla Turner | 41? | |

1854 White's Directory list Samuel Agus as a farmer.
1851 Halvergate Census:
Entry No. 111

| | | |
|---|---|---|
| Samuel Agus | 42 | widower / farmer, occupier of marshland |
| Abigail Marshall | 17 | housekeeper |
| Samuel Marshall | 6 | visitor |

1842 Tithe Apportionment lists Henry Sharman as occupant.
1841 Halvergate Census:

| | | |
|---|---|---|
| Henry Sharman | 45 | marsh farmer |
| Elizabeth Sharman | 30 | |
| Susan Shuckford | 15 | |
| Susan Shuckford | 60 | |
| Robert Brown | 10(?) | |
| Phoebe Davison | 10(?) | |

## BERTIE HIGH

Bertie Donald High was born on the 18th July 1918 the eighth and last child of James Thomas High and Nellie Howard High. His eldest brother was Harold, then there was Isabel followed by Stanley, James, Margery, Girtie, and Fred. Brother Stanley worked for the millwright Isaac Hewitt who lived at Berney Arms, and James worked for the marshman Ben Howard. Later Stanley and James together went to live at Seven Mile mills by the river Yare near Reedham. Fred worked on the Berney Arms marshes, then became a milkman on a farm in Reedham and eventually went to live down the Haddiscoe New Cut as a marshman.

Bertie, like his brothers and sisters, went to school at Reedham. This involved a walk of about a mile across the marshes to Berney Arms railway station to catch the train to Reedham, then another mile walk from the station to the school.

Every Saturday Bertie's mother and father went to Yarmouth to get groceries and cattle feed for the coming week. This was by pony and trap. There were 13 gates to open and close along the marsh track, and this was young Bertie's job. Once on the Acle New Road they were about 3 miles from Yarmouth. They would only have about ten motorcars pass them on the Acle New Road as they made that three-mile trip. If the weather was bad and there was snow and ice they would go by pony and trap across the marshes to the Berney Arms station and get a train to Yarmouth.

Apart from being a marshman, Bertie's father also kept his own cows which were milked twice a day. The milk was put through a cream separator, and the cream was stored till Thursday, when it was put into a butter churn. The butter was sold to customers in Great Yarmouth, and some went to grocers for resale. The skimmed milk was given to the young calves and when they were older Bertie's father would take them to Acle cattle market, sell them and buy more calves. The young calves would be taken home by horse and cart with a net over them so they would not fall off.

There was no drinking water only that which was collected from a galvanised roof. If the family ran out of water through lack of rain they would go about two and a half miles to Halvergate and get water from a deep well which was at Bertie's aunts place. His aunt was Phoebe wife to Sidney George Brister. There was no electric. Paraffin lamps and candles were used to show the way to bed. The coal fire was the only way to get any heat, for their cooking they used a walloven and for washdays there was a copper with a fire underneath. Coal was delivered to the Acle New Road by the coal merchants Bessey and Palmer. They would not go across the marshes, and Bertie's family had to collect it from the roadside and cart it home by horse and tumbrill.

An entry from Bertie's father's cashbook is given below.

# THE HALVERGATE FLEET : PAST & PRESENT

### 1900 Mr N H Mack

| | £ | s | d |
|---|---|---|---|
| Looking after 66 acres at 1/6 per acre | 4 | 19 | 0 |
| Stubbing and mowing thistles on marshes | 1 | 13 | 0 |
| Drawing dykes and drains 63 score at 1/6 per score | 4 | 14 | 6 |
| Fresh water rate | | 8 | 3 |
| Two journeys to Acle with bullocks | | 5 | 0 |
| One journey to Freethorpe with colts | | 1 | 0 |
| Pulling mare out of dyke | | 2 | 0 |
| Mole rate | | 8 | 3 |
| | 12 | 11 | 0 |

### 1901 Mrs Gilbert

| | £ | s | d |
|---|---|---|---|
| One year working the Mill | 5 | 2 | 0 |
| Grease and oil for Mill | | 7 | 6 |
| Bottomfying 54.5 rod of Dyke at 1/6 | 4 | 1 | 9 |
| | 9 | 11 | 3 |

Bertie remembers when he was about 10 years of age one of the cattle owners would often ask his father to take two fat cattle to Beach station Great Yarmouth or to Acle station. When they went to Beach station they would drove the cattle over the marshes through the 13 gates and go along the Acle New Road where hardly any motor vehicles would be seen.They would return home by walking to Vauxhall station where they got the train to Berney Arms and then walk the mile across the marshes home.

Another example from his father's cash book is given here

### 1928

| | £ | s | d |
|---|---|---|---|
| Moving cattle for M W Falk | | | |
| Journey to Beach Station after cattle | | 7 | 0 |
| 2 Journeys to Reedham station after cattle | | 10 | 0 |
| 3Journeys to Acle station with cattle | | 15 | 0 |
| 3 Journeys to Beach station with cattle | 1 | 1 | 0 |
| 2 Journeys to Acle station with cattle | | 10 | 0 |
| 8 Journeys to and from Fred's | | 8 | 0 |
| Paid telegram | | | 6 |
| Carrying out cake to cattle 6.25 tons | 3 | 2 | 6 |

Bertie learned to swim in a dyke when he was about 12 years old.

There were lots of bad winters when the dykes froze up, and after the animals had been sorted out Bertie would go ice skating to Halvergate. One time he skated along Branch Road to the Stracey Arms and then along the New Road to Acle and back.

**Figure 33 Cows by High's Mill in the 1930's. Courtesy of Bertie High.**

**Figure 34 Milking time. Elsie High bringing in the cows in the early 1940's.
Photo supplied by Bertie High.**

# THE HALVERGATE FLEET : PAST & PRESENT

Bertie left school in July 1932 two weeks before the August holidays because his father needed help with the haymaking. Hay was cut with a grass cutter drawn by two horses. They only owned one horse and borrowed another from people in Wickhampton. They borrowed it at the time of year when the owner did not need it. Bertie remembers his dad buying this grass cutter from Randells of North Walsham. It was delivered by train to the Reedham station and they had to go and collect it. They had to go along the Fleet marsh track to Halvergate, then through Freethorpe to get to Reedham and they towed the grass cutter behind the horse and cart all the way back home.

Hay was turned by hand until it was dry enough to rake, horse drawn into rows, then cocked or heaped up. The hay was then taken, by horse and tumbril to make a stack near the house, to be used as cattle food for the winter months.

In the autumn after the stock had left the level, which was about 300 acres, the main work was looking after the mill and dyke drawing. Dyke drawing was done with a 'shore cutter', which was like a scythe, and was used for cutting the edge of the dyke and then a 'meg' was used, and the weeds were pulled out. Another job was drain cleaning. This was done with a shore cutter, made from a stack knife fitted to a long handle, which was used to cut each side of the drain. A wooden drain tool was then used to scoop out the drain.

Nowadays dyke drawing is done with a mechanical digger, and drains are made using a tractor pulling a V-shaped drain cutter.

In the spring sometimes they would be asked to clean the dykes out, this was known as 'bottomfying'. The dykes had to be 9 feet across the top and 4 foot 6 inches across the bottom. This was a strenuous job. A mud dam would be made at each end of the stretch to be bottomfied. The edges would then be cut back with a shore cutter and then the water bailed out. The mud from the edges was then cromed out and then they would get into the bottom of the dyke with a wooden scoop and dig it out to a depth of 3 feet. When this stretch was done the back dam would be taken out and the next stretch dammed up and the process repeated.

In spring some marsh owners who had their own cattle would have them brought down to the marshes, other marshes were let at a marsh auction to the highest bidder. The cattle were usually delivered to Acle, Reedham or Great Yarmouth stations where cattle drovers met them and took them to the marshes where they would spend the summer months grazing. From time to time the cattle would be moved from one marsh to another for fresh grass. The marshman would go around the marshes twice a day to count the animals and check they were ok.

Through the summer months thistle mowing was done with a scythe.

When Bertie left school he got 5 shillings a week wages from his father, who was the official marshman on the level. When he turned 16 his wages were increased to 6 shillings. At this time he did some bottomfying to earn extra money and he used it to buy his own calves, which he reared and later sold.

Bertie started to go shooting at the age of 15. This took up all of his spare time and eventually he bought his own 8-bore gun, which was good for geese.

**Figure 35 Bertie High on his Francis Barnet in 1936. Photo from Bertie High.**

**Figure 36 Bertie High with sister Margery and Jack Carter in the late 1930's. High's marsh house is in the background and the mill is behind the trees. From Bertie High.**

During the war years Pettits of Reedham would buy almost anything, plovers, Lapwings, Starlings and even Seagulls. Starlings were bought at two old pence each. One day a week everything Bertie had caught would be put into sacks and put onto the train at Berney Arms to go to Pettits of Reedham, Pettits would pay the carriage.

Bertie bought an old motor bike, stripped off the mudguards etc. and spent many hours riding about the marshes. In 1936 he passed his driving test and was then able to drive on the proper roads. Each springtime he would buy a second hand motorbike, use it till the autumn and then sell it.

Eventually Bertie met his wife to be and they were married at St Peters church in Great Yarmouth 23 October 1943. For a short time before they were married Elsie went to live and work as a dairymaid at High's marsh house. During the war years Elsie's brother would go to the marsh house to get a good nights sleep away from the bombs falling on Yarmouth. A few bombs did land on the marshes and Bertie recalls one that fell about a hundred yards from the mill.

Bertie was called up for the home guard and went twice a week to either Halvergate or Freethorpe.

Bertie's father retired as marshman shortly after Bertie and Elsie were married, and Bertie then became the official marshman.

While Bertie and Elsie were living by the Fleet the first of their nine children was born on April 1945 at Elsie's mother's house, he was named Micheal Bertie High.

Later that year on 11th October Bertie, Elsie and baby Micheal moved from the Fleet to Potter Heigham where Bertie took over from his brother Harold as the marshman working the electric pump.

Lenny Carter from Lockgate Mill moved into High's marsh house as the new marshman here on the Fleet.

Mole catching in the 1940's was paid by the acre and skins were sold for two or three old pence each.

**Figure 37 Lenny Carter, last man to work High's mill.
Photo taken circa 1982 when he was in his 90's. Courtesy of EDP.**

**Figure 38 Wes Tooley and Bertie High photographed at The Ship Hotel, Reedham, 16th September 2001 after the Berney Arms reunion. In the 1930's they often worked together slubbing out dykes. Photograph by Paul Hutchinson.**

**Figure 39 Howard's mill in full working order. Peter Allard.**

**Figure 40 Howard's mill in 1974 and on the right in 1988. From Arthur C Smith.**

**7. HOWARD'S MILL** TG463073 South Walsham (St. Lawrence) Detached Parish; South Walsham Marshes; on the Fleet. It is also known as **SOUTH WALSHAM MILL**.

A mill was marked on Faden's map of 1797, and Bryant's map of 1826 shows a 'South Walsham' mill at this approximate location and a house nearby marked as 'Hewetts'. This was probably a miss-spelling of the name Hewitt.

The origins of the mill are unknown but the present mill was probably a rebuild, done around 1880. The tower predates the iron machinery by about 40 years, so the tower may have been built about 1840.
The windshaft had a twelve-inch drain neck, a removable tail-section and eleven-inch wide stock canisters. The headwheel was in two pieces, made of iron and was clamped around the shaft with a taper key. It was 7 feet 2 inches and drove a 5 feet diameter wallower with iron teeth which was mounted onto the upright shaft with a taper key. The upright shaft was 8 inches in diameter and made from three sections. The pitwheel was 8 feet in diameter with applewood teeth.

At ground level rough brickwork of the previous tower can be seen and in places the present brickwork does not align with the old footings.
The mill is a tarred Red Brick Tower, 3 storeys high, about 30 ft to the curb, with 2 doors and 2 windows on each upper level. It had 4 patent sails, an 8-bladed fantail and Norfolk boat-shaped cap. Each sail had 8 bays, double shuttered, with 3 vanes each, giving 48 vanes

per sail. The sails were about 25feet long and 7 ft 6inches wide.

It had a 16 feet scoop-wheel, with the inscription Smihdale & Sons on the scoop-wheel gate. There were 32 floats and they were 7 inches wide. The brick culvert was about 8 inches wide and was rebuilt in the 1930's.

It has cast iron sheer extensions supporting the fly frame, worm shaft and decking. The cap, flyframe and sails were by W.T. England.

The main machinery was by Robert Barnes of Southtown about 1880.

Some iron floor supports bear the name W. T. England Yarmouth 1911.

The following initials were found on the woodwork: AJT 1904 (A.J.Thrower), JWT, AK England, WA England 1924, R Want 1934, on the sluicegate: 'Smithdale', and on the upright shaft 'H.H. R.B. W.F.1898'.


The mill was last worked in 1947 using only 2 sails, after 2 of the sails were taken down and possibly used elsewhere. Ben Howard was the last marshman to work the mill. It remained derelict for several years.


The mill, and marshes, was owned by Lady Stracey, and later the mill was bought by Richard Seago in 1978 from Fairhaven Estates.

Richard Seago began repairing the mill with the help of grants from the Broads Authority.

The cap was blown off in Jan 1978 and Seago put a temporary corrugated metal sheet roof on top. Repairs to the mill were carried out during the 1980's, new windows and doors were in place by the summer of 1985, and in September of 1985 the windshaft with one pair of dilapidated sails and cap frame were lifted off by crane. The cap was taken away to South Walsham and the windshaft left on site. Construction of the new cap frame used English Oak and Pitch Pine for the main structure and the new fly frame was made of pitch pine. By spring 1989 the new frame was ready for transportation to the mill. A new set of truck wheels had been cast, and the cast-iron curb had been sandblasted and painted before the cap was fitted.

The new cap and fantail were fitted on 29th August 1989.

Boarding the cap took place in September 1989 with assistance of the millwright Vincent Pargeter. After this the brickwork was re-pointed and refaced.

New floors and an internal overhaul of the machinery was carried out in 1995.

Richard Seago put the mill up for sale in April 2001 with a price tag of £32,000.

In July 2001 an offer by Mr K. Halifax of Thorpe Abbot was accepted.


The **Marsh House** stands to the east of the mill. TG464072.

It is thought to have been built in the seventeenth century and had three bedrooms.

It was shown on the 1826 map as 'Hewetts'.

It is now known as 'Marsh Farm, Berney Arms'.

It is built of brick with a thatched roof. It now has a private cesspit, its own electricity generator and water is obtained from a spring.

Figure 41 Howard's house taken March 1969 by Peter Allard.

**Occupants:**

Billy Lacey was marshman in mid/ late1950's for a few years until about 1963-4. He then moved to Stone's marsh-bungalow after Fred Carter left.

The house was sold about 1964 to Brian Gibson, and later occupied by Michael Douglas who is still there. The house is up for sale at the time of writing with an asking price of £180,000.

In the 1891 South Walsham (St. Lawrence) Census:
Entry No. : On Yarmouth Marshes:

| | | |
|---|---|---|
| John Howard | 48 | Marshman (also called Ben) |
| Harriet E. Howard | 32 | wife |
| Benjamin Howard | 16 | son |
| George Howard | 5 | |
| Bertie Howard | 3 | |
| Ernest Howard | 1mth. | |
| Harriet Ellis | 16 | visitor |
| Mary Ann Teasdak | 15 | Dom. Servant |

1883 Kelly's Directory: South Walsham (St. Lawrence) Ben Howard is listed as a cowkeeper.

1881 South Walsham (St. Lawrence) Census
Entry No. 55 Marsh house on level

| | | |
|---|---|---|
| John Howard | 38 | marshman |
| Maria Howard | 37 | wife |
| Laura Howard | 12 | |
| Phoebe Howard | 10 | |
| Ben Howard | 6 | |
| John Howard | 4 | |
| Hubert Howard | 1 | |

1871 South Walsham (St. Lawrence) Census
Entry No. 43 Marsh house

| | | |
|---|---|---|
| Benjamin Howard | 28 | Marshman 10 acres |
| Maria Howard | 27 | wife |
| Laura Maria Howard | 2 | |
| Phoebe Amy Howard | 1mth | |
| Harriet Waters | 15 | servant |

1864 White's Directory lists Edward Hewitt as a farmer.

1861 South Walsham (St. Lawrence) Census
Entry No 51

| | | |
|---|---|---|
| Edward Hewitt | 56 | marsh farmer 110 acres (was at 6-mile house, Chedgrave Parish, on the Island) |
| Esther Ann Hewitt | 55 | wife (dies May 1861, buried Halvergate) |
| Sarah Hewitt | 25 | |

| Isaac Hewitt | 14 | |
|---|---|---|
| Edward Hewitt | 5 | gndson |
| Mary Ann Broome | 16 | gen servant |

1851 South Walsham (St. Lawrence) census
Entry No. 35

| Edward Hewitt | 70 | farmer / marshman, employs 1 man |
| (widower) | | |
| Elizabeth Hood | 23 | housekeeper / granddaughter |
| Mary A. Hood | 17 | granddaughter |
| Barzillia Ives | 23 | Ag. Lab./ marshman |
| Elizabeth Hales | 16 | |

1845 White's Directory list Edward Hewitt as farmer in this parish
1841 South Walsham (St. Lawrence) census

| Edward Hewitt | 60 | marshman |
| Elizabeth Hewitt | 50 | wife |
| Elizabeth Hewitt | 15 | |
| Mary Hewitt | 70 | Ind. |

**Figure 42 Billy Lacey sheep shearing at marsh farm in 1962. Photo supplied by Billy Lacey.**

## BILLY LACEY

Billy Lacey was a marshman who lived at the marsh house for a few years in the 1950's. The house at that time had downstairs two big rooms and one small room, and upstairs three bedrooms, one of which had a slanting roof. There was also an outside backplace.

He had a generator for running a D.C. television. This was a two-stroke engine and ran on petrol and paraffin. It had two fuel tanks, a small tank which had half a pint of petrol and a main tank which contained the paraffin. The engine would be started on petrol and when warm switched to paraffin. Afore Billy decided to go to bed he would switch the engine back to petrol and there would be enough fuel to last till he went to kip. When the petrol ran out the generator stopped and the television would go off.

Calor gas was used for the lights, and they had a Rayburn cooking stove in one room and an open coal fire in another room. The toilet was outside and was a three-seater.

There was no running water on tap. Rainwater was collected in tanks running down from the roof guttering, and they had a tin bath. Billy would also go to Yarmouth with his horse and cart, travelling across the marshes to Vauxhall Station, where there was a tap he could use to fill his churns with water and then take them home.

Billy's eldest son Peter went to school at Halvergate. A bus would pick him up on the Acle New Road. His daughter Susan came to the marshes when she was three days old.

Telegrams were delivered by Betty Carter from the Wickhampton Post Office and the post and the newspapers were delivered by Henry Hewitt, 'Yoiton', from the Berney Arms. One day 'Yoiton' was sniffing at his snuff and offered Jack Childs some. Jack had a couple of pinches and it nearly took his hair off he reckon.

They went shopping once a week, crossing the marshes in a pony and trap to the Acle New Road where they would get a lift into Yarmouth. Sometimes they would walk to Berney Arms Station and catch the train to Yarmouth

During the late 1950's telephone cables were taken across the marshes. John Kemp and Jack Elliot, who lived at Great Yarmouth were installing the telephone at Howard's house and each morning when they came back to restart the work the cables had been chewed through by the coypus.

## BEN HOWARD

Ben Howard kept his own cows and used the milk to make butter.

Ben and his wife had a stall on the Yarmouth Market for several years.

Ben's wife was called Sarah, and his sister-in-law, who lived with them, was Christine.

My grandfather 'Yoiton' lived-in with the Howard family before WW1 when he worked for Mr Jimmy Goffin.

Mr Jack Childs worked for a time on the marshes for Ben Howard.

Memories from Trevor Dyble who worked for the riverboard:-

One cold day Ben Howard invited some of the River Board men in for a 'hot meal'. What he served up was a raw onion for each of them.

Ben Howard often wore a sack around his shoulders and another around his waist. At the start of the sugar beet season he would get two new sacks from Cantley. When Cantley chimney began to smoke people would say 'Ben will be getting his new suit soon'.

One winter's day when Trevor and his workmates were passing Ben's place to go to work they noticed a trail in the snow looking as though something had been dragged towards Ben's house. They followed the trail up to the house and found Ben lying frozen outside his door. He had fallen into a dyke when crossing a ligger to take feed to some horses and he had crawled out of the dyke and crawled home but was exhausted and unable to reach the door handle. There was scratch marks on the paint, what little there was of it, where his nails had scratched trying to reach the handle. The Riverboard men dragged Ben inside, lit a fire and the foreman said 'He'll be thawed out by dinnertime', so they left him. He was ok and was up and about the next day.

**Figure 43 Coypu. Photo by Paul Hutchinson.**

**Figure 44 Goffin's mill in working order. Photo from Peter Allard.**

**8. GOFFIN'S MILL**, TG464070, Halvergate Parish; Halvergate Marshes; on the Fleet Dyke. This mill was also known as **MINISTER'S MILL, WALPOLE'S MILL** and sometimes as **HEWITT'S MILL** after the owners and/or marshman who lived in the nearby marsh house and worked the mill.

Figure 45 Goffin's house in the
1950's when the Everson family was
living there.
Photo supplied by Margaret Durham

Figure 46 Henry Everson
in 1956 at the wedding of
Ray Brister and Sylvia Mallet
Photo supplied by Ray Brister.

A mill was marked on Faden's map, 1797, at this location, and a mill, not named, was shown at this approximate location on Bryant's map of 1826. Also a mill was marked on the 1839 HalvergateTithe map at this location.

It is possible that the mill was rebuilt or altered over the years.

The last structure standing was a typical brick tower mill with 4 patent sails, each with 9 bays, double-shuttered, 3 per bay, giving 54 shutters per sail.

It had a fantail with 8 blades, and a boat-shaped cap and drove an external scoopwheel. It is believed to have been built or rebuilt by Stolworthy.

The mill was last worked by Fred Hewitt, in about 1948, and it was demolished in the 1950's. The brick rubble was used to fill the ruts in the marsh gateways. The site is still visible with a pile of bricks and rubble and some remains of the sluice.

In 1842 Tithe Apportionment the mill and landowner was Sir Edward Walpole Esq.

The mill was owned by Myrus Sutton, in 1930's & 40's, and Sutton was listed in 1937 Kelly's Directory as a 'Farmer and Cattle Dealer' at Halvergate.

The **Marsh House** stands a few yards to the east of the mill. TG465070.

It is believed to be late seventeenth century built. It was shown on Bryant's map as **Walpole's** Farm in 1826, and was shown on the 1839 Halvergate map. It still exists and is known as Fleet Farm, Berney Arms. The house has two rooms upstairs and is thatched.

**Occupants:**
FRED NICHOLS was last marshman at the house, he was nicknamed 'Mauky'. His wife was called Pauline. The house remained empty for a while after he left in 1966 and is now owned by Mr F. Futter and is known as 'Fleet Farm, Berney Arms'.

**Figure 47 Fred 'Mauky' Nichols, the last marshman to live at Goffin's marsh house. Photograph supplied by Peter Allard.**

Henry Everson and his wife Violet, lived here at the time of the 1953 floods. Violet was a Webster and was daughter of Jimmy Webster at Wickhampton. Jimmy Webster worked a small holding near to Church Farm. Henry Everson worked as a drover for Sutton before he went to live here.
We find the following information documented:
1937 Kelly's Directory:    Fred Hewitt       Marshman
1916 Kelly's Directory lists James Goffin    Marshman       (Note He was buried at Wickhampton Church, having died 16th January 1945 aged 86. His wife Elizabeth died 18th December 1928 aged 66.)
1891 Halvergate Census:
Entry No. 117. On the Marshes:

| | | |
|---|---|---|
| James Minister | 87 | Marshman (born. 10 July 1808, d. 28Oct 1893) |
| Hannah Minister | 85 | wife (born 1805, died Mar. 1892, bur. Wickhampton) |
| William Minister | 51 | son / Marshman |
| Charlotte Fake | 44 | widow/ daughter |
| Martha Fake | 10 | granddaughter |
| James High | 19 | grandson / Marshman (he later worked High's Mill and dies 15 Oct 1953) |
| Hetty Want | 17 | servant |

1881 Halvergate Census:
Entry No. 48 Marsh house

| | | |
|---|---|---|
| James Minister | 77 | Marsh farmer |
| Hannah Minister | 75 | wife |
| William Minister | 41 | Marshman |
| Elizabeth Hewitt | 18 | grand daughter / visitor (probably a daughter of James & Ann Hewitt) |

1871 Halvergate Census
Entry No. 99

| | | |
|---|---|---|
| James Minister | 67 | Marsh farmer 50 acres |
| Hannah Minister | 65 | wife |
| William Minister | 32 | Marshman |
| Harriet Newson | 13 | niece |

1861 Halvergate Census
Entry No 109

| | | |
|---|---|---|
| James Minister | 57 | marshman |
| Hannah Minister | 55 | |
| Mary Minister | 25 | |
| William Minister | 21 | marshman |
| Ann Minister | 19 | (later becomes Mrs James Hewitt) |
| Charlotte Minister | 15 | (later becomes Mrs Fake) |
| Harriet Newson | 2 | gnddaughter |

1851 Halvergate Census
Entry No. 112

| | | |
|---|---|---|
| James Minister | 47 | farmer occupier of marshland |
| Hannah Minister | 43 | wife |
| Mary Minister | 15 | |
| Harriet Minister | 13 | |
| William Minister | 11 | |
| Ann Minister | 8 | |
| Robert Minister | 7 | |
| Charlotte Minister | 5 | |
| William Harper | 61 | lodger |

1841 Halvergate Census

| | | |
|---|---|---|
| James Minister | 35 | Marshman |
| Hannah Minister | 35 | |
| Elizabeth Minister | 15 | |
| James Minister | 13 | (dies 24 Dec 1898-wife was Harriet) |
| Hannah Minister | 10 | |
| Mary Minister | 6 | |
| Harriet Minister | 4 | |
| William Minister | 2 | |

**Figure 48 Three views of Goffin's house. Photographs March 1969 by Peter Allard.**

## FRED HEWITT

Old Fred Hewitt, once a fisherman, lived here during the 1930's-40's with his second wife Hannah, but after his wife left him he took live-in housekeepers. One of these was Hilda Morter. Phylis Neave, Hilda's niece went to stay at the marsh house during her holidays as a young girl in the 1940's.

He was referred to as old Fred because he had a son, young Fred, who lived nearby at Berney Arms for several years.

Fred was a marshman who looked after his own level, counting the cattle, dyke drawing, drain cleaning, and thistle topping. He was also working Goffin's Mill at this time and in the 1937 Kelly's Directory he was listed as a Marshman. He was well known for the onions he grew.

The house had two rooms downstairs, one known as the best room. The other had a coal fire cooking range and a copper with a fire underneath which was used to do the washing. There was a long dairy with a water pump, which was used for pumping water from the well, and there was another smaller dairy further away. They drank water from the Fleet and also rain water from the roof, which came from the guttering into a tank. When their water was low they had Churns of water brought from Yarmouth by train to Berney Arms Station, and they would collect them using a horse and cart.

There was no electricity; candles and mantle lamps were used for lights.

Fred Hewitt had chickens and cows and Hilda made butter. They also collected mushrooms off the marshes. Fred and Hilda would go by horse and cart to Yarmouth to sell their produce to the market stall holders.

Every Saturday when mushrooms were in season Hilda would load her bike with bags of mushrooms and make the trip to Berney Arms station to get the train to Yarmouth. Getting a bike over a ligger was very tricky especially when loaded up, and Hilda tumbled into the dyke with mushrooms going everywhere on more than one occasion.

Hilda went to Yarmouth every Saturday to do the grocery shopping and always called into Docwras sweet shop in the Market Row, before going home on the Berney Arms train. On one occasion the train stopped short of the station platform and not realising, she stepped backwards off the train and fell to the ground with her sweets and groceries going everywhere.

During the war years Millie High was the Berney Arms post-woman and delivered mail to the marsh house.

Fred Hewitt and Hilda Morter would go to all the Methodist Sunday School anniversaries. It was a good day out going to Halvergate, Freethorpe and Wickhampton.

Fred Hewitt was responsible for looking after about 550 acres and was responsible to thirteen masters, including Mr Denny Wright who bred Suffolk colt horses.

Fred owned 60 acres of his own.

Coal was delivered once a year by lorry in the summer months when the weather was good.

Fred liked his drink and one tale is told that walking home 'worse for wear' he fell into a

deep dyke. It was too steep for him to climb out so he walked the length of the dyke in the water till he got near home when he then climbed out.
When Fred left the Fleet he moved to a small holding at Hickling.

**Figure 49 Fred Hewitt and his wife Hannah at the door to the marsh house.**
**Fred was well known for the onions he grew.**
**Photo supplied by Bob and Violet Mace.**

**BREYDON PUMP** TG477070

The Fleet entered the Breydon Water via a Sluice Gate. When the Fleet was full and the tide was low the sluice gates would be opened to allow the Fleet to empty.
In 1934 the Diesel Pump was brought on line. It was capable of pumping 35 tons/ min.

An electric pump was built, starting in 1946 and was officially opened in October 1948 by Mr H. Gardiner assistant secretary of the Ministry of Agriculture and Fisheries. Myrus Sutton was Vice-Chairman of the Internal Drainage Board in the 1940's when the Elec. Pump was opened.

It could pump at 80 tons/min. The plant was installed by Thomas Smithdale & Sons and the electricity supply was provided by the Eastern Electricity Board.
The Fleet was deepened when the new electric pump was built.
This made the windmills on the Fleet redundant and the new pump maintained the levels of the Fleet dyke sufficiently low so as the marshes drained by gravity regulated by sluices.

Some Operators of the pump were:
Fred Hewitt, living at Goffin's mill house, worked the pump in the 1930's & 40's, and his son young Fred Hewitt when living at Berney Arms. Reggie Mace also worked the pump when he was working for Fred Hewitt.
Henry Hewitt, 'Yoiton', when he lived at Berney Arms, and after he had moved to Cobholm, worked the pump, and he was followed by his son Stanley Hewitt for a few years from 1964.

**Figure 50 Henry Bumbury Hewitt 'Yoiton' at the Breydon pumphouse in 1964.
Photo from Peter Allard.**

Figure 51 A gathering at the official opening of the Breydon pump in 1948. Photo supplied by Phylis Neave.

**Figure 52 The Breydon Pump 1948. From the left is Fred Hewitt, David Wright, Myrus Sutton, Unidentified, Gordon Addison, Henry Preston(?), Joe Kerry, Billy Key, Michael Wright, Unidentified. Photo from Phylis Neave.**

**LOCKGATE MILL** TG480072    Freethorpe Detached Parish.
This is also Known as **Freethorpe Mill**, **Banham's Black Mill** and **Duffel's Mill**.

This Mill is not on the Halvergate Fleet but drains its own marshes. It is located only a few yards from the Breydon Pump.
It was not marked on Faden's map of 1797 but was marked on Bryant's map of 1826 as Freethorpe Mill.
The mill is four storeys high, built in red brick and tarred black. The brickwork stands thirty five feet high. It is about 24 feet overall diameter at the base and had four windows and two doors. It carried four patent sails, which turned clockwise and drove a large external scoop wheel, 19 feet in diameter with seven-inch wide paddles.
When it was put up for sale in 1877 it was described as 'recently erected by Smithdales of Acle' so the existing mill was probably a rebuild.
A small steam engine was installed in the early 1900's for a time. Arthur Patterson mentioned the engine in his book of 1907 and said Dan Banham was the marshman.
Bob Banham operated the mill around 1912 and Gordon Addison, who lived at nearby Lockgate Farm, is believed to have looked after the mill for a time in the 1920's.
The mill was last worked in about 1947 by Leonard Carter.
The mill remained derelict and the sails were blown down in 1953.
A temporary aluminium cap was fitted in 1985.

**Figure 53 Lockgate Mill in working order and marsh house on the left.**

In November 1988 the mill, and the derelict marsh house, then owned by the Banham family, went up for sale and was bought by Mr Kim Baker for £16,000.
The mill is still owned by Mr Baker.

There was a fire at the mill in April 2001, probably caused by vandals. Because of the foot and mouth restrictions imposed at the time the fire engine sent to the fire had to wait on the concrete road for someone to come along to disinfect it, before it could go across the marsh track to the mill.

**Marsh House** TG480072. This stands next to the mill
The marsh house had a tiled roof and was built of Suffolk whites bricks, and was tarred black the same as the mill. Dorothy Hanton, nee Carter, recalls that the marsh house had two bedrooms upstairs and two living rooms downstairs. The kitchen was built separate and you had to go outside to get to it. It also had a dairy. There was no electricity so they used a primus stove for boiling the kettle, and candles, Tilley lamps and Mantle lamps for light. Cooking was done with a coal-fired cooking range. Water was obtained from the roof and collected in tanks, and washing was done in a copper.

Jack French, who worked for the Banham family, lived here with his family for a few years before 1952 and again after the 1953 floods for a while (they lived in the cottages at Berney Arms in 1952-3) The damaged red pine sails of the mill were laying beside the mill and they used them for firewood.
Jack French had a goat when he lived here. One day the goat got onto the nearby railway line and charged at an oncoming train and was killed. Ben Banham buried the goat not far from the marsh house but left the horns sticking out of the ground. Jack had to dig it up and rebury it.
Lenny Rose occupied the marsh house for a short period before the French family.
Len Carter was here from 1931 till about 1945 and was last marshman to work the mill.
Jimmy Banham lived here before Len Carter according to Ernest Hewitt, a cousin to Jimmy Banham, and in the 1937 Kelly's directory a Mr James Banham is listed as marshman for Freethorpe, but Len Carter was in residence at that time.

The following information is found in the Freethorpe Censuses and is believed to refer to Lockgate Marsh House.

1891 Freethorpe Census
| Entry No. 96 | | (Lockgate Mill Marsh house) |
|---|---|---|
| Daniel Banham | 38 | marshman |
| Jane Banham | 38 | wife |
| Margaret Banham | 18 | |
| Mary A. Banham | 16 | |
| Christiana Banham | 12 | |
| George Smith | 15 | marshman / lodger |
| Entry No. 97 | | (May be Lockgate Farm. Must be close to railway !) |
| John Smith | 63 | marshman |

| | | |
|---|---|---|
| Eliza Smith | 63 | |
| Fred Smith | 21 | marshman |
| Susana Smith | 18 | |
| Charles Garwood | 5 | nephew |
| Edward Hanton | 17 | lodger / railway lab. |
| 1881 Freethorpe Census | | |
| Entry No. 1 marsh house | | (Lockgate Mill Marsh house) |
| Daniel Key Banham | 28 | marshman (a son of Last Banham) |
| Jane Anna Banham | 28 | (nee Smith?) |
| Betsy Banham | 8 | |
| Susan Mary Ann Banham | 6 | |
| Sarah Ann Banham | 40 | |
| Christiana Jane Banham | 2 | |
| Un-named Banham | 5days | |
| Jane Banham | 17 | |
| Margaret Jones | 20 | sister |
| Herbert Jones | 1mth | |
| 1871 Freethorpe Census | | |
| Entry No 99 | | (Lockgate Mill Marsh house) |
| George Smith | 51? | Marsh farmer |
| Mary Ann Smith | 40 | |
| Fred Smith | 19 | millwright |
| Mary Ann Smith | 11 | |
| Samuel or Daniel? Smith | 4 | |
| William Smith | 3 | |
| Jane Thaxter | 16 | servant |
| William Pigmy | 40 | dom serv |
| Sam Clark | 30 | lodger / lab |
| Elizabeth Clark | 27 | |
| 1861 Freethorpe Census | | |
| Entry No 1 | | (Lockgate Mill Marsh house) |
| George Smith | 41 | marsh farmer |
| Mary Ann Smith | 31 | |
| Fred Smith | 12 | |
| Mary Ann Smith | 6 | |
| Sarah A. Browne | 21 | dairymaid |
| Tabitha Banham | 18 | housemaid (probably daughter of Ben Banham then living at Ashtree farm on Acle New Rd.) |
| 1851 Freethorpe Census | | |
| Entry No. 22 | | (Lockgate Mill Marsh house) |
| George Smith | 30 | marshman / ag. Lab. |
| Mary Ann Smith | ? | |

Fred Clark                          ?
1841 Freethorpe Census                    (Lockgate Mill Marsh house)
John Withers                   35   marshman
Mary Withers                   35   wife
George Smith                   15
Martha Tary(?)                 20

**Figure 54 'Yoiton' and Ben Banham at AshTree Farm Berney Arms. Ben had AshTree Farm on the Acle New Road and employed Len Carter and Jack French when they lived in Lockgate Marsh house. Photo from Sid Gibbs.**

## PERCY HEWITT

Percy Hewitt worked for the Lower Bure, Halvergate Fleet and Acle Marshes Internal Drainage Board cleaning out the drainage dykes, of which there was about 75 miles, using a mechanical digger. Every dyke would be cleaned out with the digger about every four or five years.

One day working on the Fleet dyke the soil gave way under the digger and it fell into the dyke. Luckily for Percy the door landed uppermost and Percy was able to get out. Brian Banham and John Fielding, Clerk to the Internal Drainage Board, fetched a tractor and winched the digger upright and Percy was able to take the digger out of the dyke.

**Figure 55 Banham's colts on marshes by Lockgate Mill in the mid 1950's.
Photograph supplied by David Pyett.**

**Figure 56 Percy Hewitt's digger in the Fleet. From Billy Lacey.**

## BRIAN GRINT

During the 1950's and 1960's when Brian was a child and teenager the Fleet was a thriving wildlife centre full of fish, frogs Harnsers, and duck. He remembers watching drovers taking cattle through Halvergate, on their way from Reedham station to the Fleet wall and then onto the marshes.

Brian is a descendant of the Mutton family and he was then living in Halvergate. He spent much of his time in those days on the marshes and on the Fleet, fishing for perch, roach and pike, gathering mushrooms and catching coypu. The coypu pelts were sold to Pettits of Reedham. He also walked the length of the Fleet wall to Breydon Water to go eel fishing. The eel catch was brought home and sold to the landlady of the Halvergate Red Lion. He and his friends also built some rafts and had great fun floating up and down the Fleet.

Brian remembers a thunderstorm in the early sixties when a crack of thunder frightened a tractor driver so much that he lost control of the wheel, steered into the Fleet and four churns full of milk emptied into the Fleet. He also remembers sheltering in Mutton's mill during a storm only to realise the best lightning conductor was right above his head.

**Figure 57 Berney Arms station about 1950 with Violet, Eliza and Albert Hewitt by the signal box. Courtesy of Alan Savory.**

## JOHN WILLIMOTT

The photograph shows Berney Arms station with Violet Hewitt, Eliza Hewitt and Albert Hewitt who lived in the station cottages standing in-front of the signal box. Many of the folk from the Halvergate Fleet caught the train here to go to Great Yarmouth or to Reedham. In those days the trains ran more frequently than they do today.

At the back of the station house there was a red telephone box. John Willmont who went to Berney Arms with Royston Mallet reed cutting, and also worked on the Berney side of the Fleet, remembers Henry Hewitt, 'Yoiton' was in the phone box trying to make a call. John was walking nearby when 'Yoiton' called out to him 'the phone don't work, I'm trying to put a bet on with John Pointon'. John phoned the operator and she asked 'has he put any money in?' 'Yes 2 pence', was the reply. The operator then said it had gone up to three pence. 'Yoiton' replied 'I did not know it was hained' (gone up).

## Appendix 1 RAILWAY COTTAGES AT 7-MILE

These cottages were built around 1844 when the Norwich Yarmouth Railway was built.
The building consisted of a terrace of three cottages, and was located in the parish of Wickhampton. The censuses listed here show that in addition to the expected railway workers, there was a marshman living in one of the cottages for most of the time. The marshman probably worked on the Wickhampton marshes and the marshes around 7 Mile House and may have been involved with the mills near to 7 Mile House.
In later years the marshman Fred High lived in one of the cottages for a while after he got married to Milly Hewitt.

**Figure 58 Derelict Railway cottages at 7-mile.**
**Photo taken 12 April 1969 by Peter Allard.**

1891 Wickhampton
Entry No. 164 (Railway Cottage at 7-mile)

| | | |
|---|---|---|
| John Burgess | 65 | Marshman |
| Harriet Burgess | 67 | |
| Ernest Hubbard | 16 | farm Lab. |

1881 Wickhampton
Entry No. 192 (Railway Cottage at 7-mile)

| | | |
|---|---|---|
| William Halesworth | 47 | Marshman |
| Rosanna Halesworth | 50 | |

1871 Wickhampton
Entry No. 1 On the railway (Railway Cottage at 7-mile)

| | | |
|---|---|---|
| William Halesworth | 37 | lab (probably a marsh lab see 1861) |
| Susanna Halesworth | 40 | |

1861 Wickhampton
Entry No 1.Railway House

| | | |
|---|---|---|
| William Halesworth | 20 | Marshman |
| Susanna Halesworth | 30 | |

1851 Wickhampton
Entry No. 1 (railway cottage)

| | | |
|---|---|---|
| Thomas Kettle | 35 | railway lab |
| Elizabeth Kettle | 42 | |
| Eliza Kettle | 7 | |
| John Burgess | 24 | lodger / marsh lab. |

## Appendix 2 OTHER MARSHMEN IN HALVERGATE & WICKHAMPTON

The following marshmen are listed in the censuses and, although not living on the Fleet, may have worked on the marshes near the Fleet.

### HALVERGATE
1891 Entry No. 67 Marsh Rd

| | | |
|---|---|---|
| Isaac Hewitt | 44 | marshman (son of Edward Hewitt/dies 13 July 1909) |
| Christiana Hewitt | 36 | |
| Stephen Hewitt | 12 | |
| Dora Hewitt | 10 | |
| Alfred Hewitt | 8 | (marries Emma Holland, later marshman at Pilson Green.) |
| Henry A. Hewitt | 6 | |
| Frederick Hewitt | 4 | |
| Nellie Hewitt | 2 | |
| Walter Hewitt | 10mths | |
| Mary Harper | | |

1881 Entry No. 4
Isaac Hewitt     34     Marshman (son of Edward Hewitt)
1871Entry No. 100
Thomas Sharman     67     Marsh Farmer
1851 Entry No. 113
Robert Turner     46     widow marshman
Louisa Turner     16     dau.
Charles Turner     5     son
1841
Barzillia Ives     45     marshman
1841
John Sheppard     70     marshman

## WICKHAMPTON

1891 Entry No. 146 The Street
James Hewitt     49     marshman (a son of Edward Hewitt)
Ann Hewitt     49
Albert Hewitt     19     wheelwright
Frederick Hewitt     8
1881 Entry No. 209
James Hewitt     39     Marshman (a son of Edward Hewitt)
Ann Hewitt     39     (nee Minister?)
James A Hewitt     16     Ag Lab
Isaac W. Hewitt     15     Ag Lab
David R. Hewitt     11     Ag Lab
Albert Hewitt     9
Ester A. Hewitt     6
1861 Entry No 27
George Burgess     33     marshman
Elizabeth Burgess     35
Harriet Burgess     10
George Burgess     4
James Burgess     2
Robert Burgess     5mths
James Minister     33     lodger/ marshman (probably the son of James Minister at Goffin's millhouse)

1851 Entry No.11
James Newson     70     marsh farmer 30 acres
Elizabeth Newson     65
1851 Entry No. 16
Robert Bullman     66     marsh farmer 30 acres
Harriet Bullman     20     daughter